LITTLE BOOK OF C*NTS

PUBLISHED BY
NUMBER NINE PUBLISHING

COPYRIGHT MAY 2018

CONTACT:
numberninepublishing@gmail.com

ISBN:
978-1-9996847-8-5
Cover: SHIELDS & YANKOWSKI
Artwork: THE AUTHOR

All rights reserved. No part of this publication may be reproduced, stored in a retrieval system, or transmitted in any form or by any means, electronic, mechanical, photocopying, recording or otherwise, without the prior permission of the copyright owner.

The author asserts copyright and retains worldwide rights.

Any similarity to c*nts you may know, or to c*nts living or dead, is purely coincidental.

CHAPTER ONE

1: Not all c*nts are men.
2: Not all c*nts are women.
3: C*nts may be found in all professions and occupations.
4: C*nts come in all shapes, shades and sizes.

5: The love of money is a major source of c*ntishness.
6: A lot of c*nts die of stupidity.
7: A c*nt will steal the ring from the hand that feeds it.

8: C*nts have rights: never 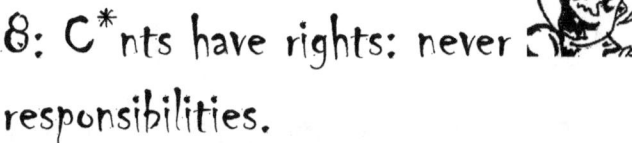 responsibilities.

9: Some c*nts believe themselves incapable of c*ntishness.

10: Today's lesson? The world is full of c*nts.

CHAPTER TWO

1: Too many encounters with c*nts may sour your perspective.

2: A c*nt pleased with your success is seeking to profit from it.

3: The c*nt is righteous. Every other c*nt is corrupt.

4: C*nts never prepare for a rainy day. C*nts prefer to steal umbrellas.

5: No one can out flatter the self-flattery of the c*nt.

6: A c*nts closest companion is envy.

7: If the last words you hear are "die c*nt die" you have probably led a life of c*ntishness.

8: C*nts are rarely cheerful.

9: C*nts delight in the faults of others.

10: C*ntishness is highly contagious.

A moment of reflection

Who is the most miserable c*nt in your life right now?

NOTES

CHAPTER THREE

1: A c*nt in the house is like hyenas circling a cadaver.

2: When a c*nt is upset everybody has to know about it.

3: C*nts are cunning. Three letter clue?

4: For three c*nts to keep a secret, two c*nts need to be dead.

5: C*nts esteem themselves limitlessly.

6: C*nts are filled with suspicion and mistrust.

7: Incapacity for gratitude? C*nt.

8: Hell is full of c*nts.

9: Some c*nts believe the most important things are things.

10: A lot of c*nts gets their history from Hollywood.

CHAPTER FOUR

1: A c*nt can be the ruination of their neighbours and neighbourhood.

2: C*nts that can't be wrong most often are.

3: A c*nts time is precious. The time of other c*nts is not.

4: C*nts gets busy delivering bad news. They have no time for hope.

5: Some c*nts never know when to shut up.

6: Feeling insecure? You've been acting the c*nt.

7: C*nt's borrow and never lend.

8: A c*nt is first out of the taxi and last into the bar.

9: Where do all the lonely c*nts come from? Where do they all belong?

10: Time eventually exposes all c*ntishness.

A moment of reflection.

Who is the c*nt that wastes most of your time?

NOTES

CHAPTER FIVE

1: C*nts of a feather flock together.

2: The affections of a c*nt are counterfeit.

3: C*nts reject wisdom.

4: Hear a lie? Listen to the c*nt.

5: Political c*nts feign interest in the populace to curry favour.

6: Anything lent to a c*nt automatically becomes a gift.

7: A c*nt will take advantage of the simple and the innocent.

8: C*nts choose cruelty over compassion.

9: C*nts bask in flattery.

10: A c*nt with knowledge seeks advantage.

CHAPTER SIX

1: Even the c*nt cannot comprehend the depth of the c*nt's own c*ntishness.

2: C*nt or full-blown c*nt? A question of degree.

3: The downfall of a c*nt delights both friends and enemies alike.

4: Once a c*nt has made a c*nt of you, you are a c*nt.

5: C*nts trick? Inciting quarrels.

6: To remain employed by a c*nt of a boss, do not point out their c*ntishness.

7: The heart of the c*nt is duplicitous.

8: C*nts are pursued by unpaid debts.

9: A c*nt will eat a starving man out of house and home even though their own cupboards groan.

10: C*nts love to sacrifice other c*nts.

A moment of reflection.

Who is the most c*ntish boss you have ever had?
What made them so c*ntish?
Why do you think they were such c*nts?

NOTES

CHAPTER SEVEN

1: C*nts live by deception.

2: A c*nt can never be corrected.

3: The more lavish the funeral; the bigger the c*nt?

4: C*nts trick? Burglary.

5: When a c*nt is ill nobody was ever as ill as that c*nt.

6: There is always time for c*ntishness.

7: The good a c*nt might do is based on the good they do themselves.

8: All interactions with a c*nt are transactions from which the c*nt wishes to gain.

9: The promise of a c*nt may as well be written on running water.

10: Certain c*nts gain medals, awards, accolades, honours and titles for their c*ntishness.

CHAPTER EIGHT

1: *No c*nt loves the c*nt more than the c*nt loves their own self.*

2: C*nts have accidents. Every other c*nt is negligent and stupid.

3: Some full-time c*nts believe themselves to be part-time c*nts.

4: C*nts always know where other c*nts went wrong — after the event.

5: A lying, cheating robbing c*nt is lying and trying to rob and cheat you when he denies being a c*nt.

6: C*ntish is as c*ntish does.

7: C*nts are generally slippery in word and deed.

8: A c*nt will suck you dry.

9: A c*nts c*ntishness is beyond the imagination of the non-c*nt.
10: See a haughty bearing? Looking at a c*nt.

A moment of reflection.

Which c*nt has ripped you off most in your life?
How did they get away with it?

NOTES

CHAPTER NINE

1: C*nts can talk themselves into anything.

2: C*nts are wise in c*ntish affairs.

3: C*nts reject advice.

4: A c*nt will wink an eye, shuffle their feet and point the finger at all the other c*nts in the town.

5: The right hand of the c*nt is duplicity. The left, deceit.

6: Never sleep when a c*nt is nearby.

7: When you have a c*nt at the table be afraid. Very afraid.

8: A c*nt is always curious about the income of other c*nts.

9: The words of a c*nt are full of murder and threats.
10: How long is the attention span of a c...?

CHAPTER TEN

1: C*nts love to have servants.
2: There are a lot of c*nts out there calling other c*nts "C*nt!"

3: C*nts see vanity in beauty.
4: If two c*nts argue for more than five minutes they are both wrong.
5: C*nts expose the faults of others and conceal their own.

6: Some c*nts are proud of their humility.

7: The first act of c*ntishness is perpetrated against the self.

8: C*nts tell hateful and disgraceful lies.

9: Regardless of appearances the c*nts devotion is to self-interest.

10: Why do so many c*nts derive so much pleasure from mockery?

CHAPTER ELEVEN

1: Some c*nts like to turn their family into servants.

2: A c*nt with insomnia is thinking up c*ntish tricks.

3: C*nts are often multi – lingual, with a sound grasp of Duplicity, Deceit and Double Tongue.

4: A bunch of c*nts, led by a c*nt, is still a bunch of c*nts.

5: C*nts can talk much and say nothing.

6: C*nts inflict unhappiness upon themselves.

7: A c*nt will take all that they can.

8: C*ntish minds fester on c*ntish issues.

9: The cowardice of the c*nt is unfathomable.

10: What sort of a c*nt has a problem with other c*nts acting the c*nt?

CHAPTER TWELVE

1: Some c*nts like to turn their servants into slaves.

2: C*ntish doctors have no interest in health.

3: Some c*nts are ashamed to admit that what they once loved now hates them.

4: C*ntishness is often camouflaged by sweet words and outward piety.

5: C*nts forget favours.

6: C*nts are intoxicated by self-importance.

7: The c*nts speech is incompatible with truth.

8: The greatest delight of the c*nt is the downfall of another c*nt.

9: C*nts persecute the good.

10: Some c*nts don't seem to know that they are c*nts.

CHAPTER THIRTEEN

1: A c*ntish wife is like cancer in the husband's bones.
2: The way of a c*nt is c*ntishness.
3: A c*nt advertises their c*ntishness by opening their mouth.
4: A c*nt will conceal their shortcomings by blaming others.
5: For four c*nts to keep a secret, three c*nts need to be dead.
6: C*nts answer favours with theft.
7: C*nts cannot endure the happiness of other c*nts.
8: 100% of f*ck all is f*ck all. C*nt!
9: C*nts despise discipline.

10: No matter how far a c*nt roams they are always in the company of a c*nt.

CHAPTER FOURTEEN

1: A c*ntish husband is like cancer in the wife's bones.

2: Every c*nt thinks himself the cleverest of c*nts.

3: A c*nt believes stolen wine tastes sweetest.

4: Some c*nts never learn.

5: C*nts love the sound of their own voices.

6: Is it possible for an honest c*nt to achieve high office?

7: Laziness and habit set the boundaries of a c*nt's learning.

8: Some c*nts believe themselves to be their own best source of advice.

9: The words of a c*nt are crooked and perverse.

10: A c*nt will dine luxuriously before a starving man.

A moment of reflection.

Who is the laziest c*nt you have ever met?

NOTES

CHAPTER FIFTEEN

1: Some c*nts are never satisfied.
2: Some c*nts get nervous when people know where they live.
3: Some sweet-talking c*nts think their words are honey — but listen closely — the sweetness is there to mask the poison.

4: If an educational system is run by c*nts for c*ntish reasons; is it any wonder that the world is full of c*nts?!

5: Some c*nts are parasites, hopping from host to host.

6: Words of rebuke are wasted on the c*nt.

7: A c*nt revels in the losses of others.

8: C*nts despise their inferiors for being inferior and hate their superiors for being superior.

9: C*nts never pay their dues.

10: When Wisdom screams from the rooftops, c*nts go deaf.

CHAPTER SIXTEEN

1: There is no honour among c*nts.

2: C*nts do not know how to be generous.

3: The c*nts eye settles on shiny things. Watch those eyes glisten.

4: C*nts shit in the river.

5: C*nts always follow the malign example.

6: Never trust the testimony of a c*nt.

7: Some crafty c*nts hide great faults by admitting a small one.

8: A crooked c*nt who makes a fortune is likely to be cheated out of it by another crooked c*nt.

9: C*nts bring sorrow upon their mothers.

10: A c*nt is like poison gas to the eyes.

A moment of reflection.

What is the most c*ntishish thing you have ever done?

NOTES

Better not use this space. Some nosey c*nt might find it and use it to make a c*nt of you.

CHAPTER SEVENTEEN

1: A c*nt of a teacher can teach nothing.

2: A c*nt claims welfare and works on the side.

3: A c*nt will drink your well dry.

4: Some c*nt is always trying to steal the foundations.

5: A c*nt likes to come between you and your family.

6: C*nts flatter themselves on their c*ntishness.

7: C*ntishness is meat and wine to a c*nt.

8: C*nts want to make everyone into c*nts like them.

9: A c*nts cheek is never kissed by the blush of shame.

10: C*nts relish the opportunity to reprimand.

CHAPTER EIGHTEEN

1: Stupid c*nts don't think about tomorrow.

2: C*nt's trick? Squandering an inheritance.

3: C*nts sling shit at virtue.

4: C*nts protect the powerful.

5: Some c*nts give bad advice because they cannot set a bad example.

6: Guns don't kill people. C*nts with guns kill people.

7: When a c*nt is sick every other c*nt must know about it.

8: Every c*nt wants to guzzle the wine; but never to tend the vine.

9: C*nts claim credit for insightful planning when they benefit from accidents.

10: What sort of a c*nt lets another c*nt make a c*nt out of them?

A moment of reflection.

What is the most c*ntish thing you have seen in the news this week?

Was it any worse than the most c*ntish thing from last week?

NOTES

CHAPTER NINETEEN

1: Give a c*nt a gun and they can rob

a bank. Give a c*nt a bank and they can rob the world.

2: The mind of a c*nt is a sealed box.

3: A c*nt knows the price of everything and the value of nothing.

4: When a c*nt attains high office, their merit should be measured by the means he used to attain it.

5: "Just doing my job, mate." The cry of the c*nt.

6: C*nts trick? Cruelty to animals.

7: C*nts never give anything of themselves.

8: Small inconveniences to the c*nt are resented more than the greatest suffering ever endured by any other c*nt.

9: A negligent c*nt leeches from the diligent.

10: Why do a lot of c*nts treat every other c*nt like a c*nt; yet, believe that they themselves should not be treated like c*nts?

CHAPTER TWENTY

1: A c*nt never forgets and never forgives.

2: C*nts can always spot the c*ntishness in others: never in themselves.

3: Offer good advice to a c*nt? Receive abuse in return.

4: Some c*nts always wants to snoop around other c*nt's homes. Especially after watching *Antiques Roadshow*.

5: If you have to tell lies about what you've been doing, you have probably been acting the c*nt.

6: Austerity for you. Conspicuous consumption for the c*nt.

7: C*nts are rarely modest about their own achievements.

8: Rich c*nts often use their money to protect themselves from the consequences of their c*ntishness.

9: A c*nt believes that charity begins and ends with the c*nt.

10: What sort of a c*nt makes a c*nt out of themselves?

A moment of reflection.

Which c*nt has told you the most lies so far in your life?

NOTES

CHAPTER TWENTY-ONE

1: When a famous c*nt dies, they soon become infamous.

2: C*ntish parents make for c*nty children.

3: The c*nts tongue pours forth lies.

4: A c*nt has money for luxury and extravagance: but none for self-examination.

5: Why are thick c*nts so intimidated by intelligent c*nts?

6: C*nts trick? The unearned increment.

7: A c*nt will always walk by.

8: Beware of eloquent c*nts. They sway others to c*ntishness.

9: C*nts, blind to their own c*ntishness are highly alert to c*ntishness in others.

10: A lot of c*nts choose to believe the convenient lie than face the inconvenient truth.

CHAPTER TWENTY-TWO

1: C*nts can peel oranges in their pocket.

2: Most c*nts are either preoccupied with the pursuit of other c*nt's money or complaining about their own.

3: A c*nt demands compensation: but offers none.

4: Drunken text asking for cash? Probably from a c*nt.

5: A c*nts hatred is more enduring than their memory of the origins of that hate.

6: A c*nt sells stolen goods on the weekly market.

7: A c*nt always has a sob story.

8: C*nts will kill your spirit and murder your soul.

9: C*ntish governments enact c*ntish laws.

10: Cancer can be cured. Can c*ntishness?

CHAPTER TWENTY-THREE

1: Some c*nts wear themselves out in the thankless service of other c*nts in order to obtain money.

2: There are songs of joy when a c*nt dies.

3: One way or another, every c*nt is exploiting some other c*nt.

4: A c*nt cannot teach another c*nt until the second c*nt is ready to learn.

5: Aggressive c*nts are usually afraid.

6: C*nts enjoy laying traps and snares for the innocent.

7: Many apparently pious c*nts: few with any humility.

8: C*nts make themselves more intelligent by keeping company with fools.

9: C*nts desire golden crowns for themselves: thorns for everyone else.
10: Some c*nts believe gadgets will make them happy.

CHAPTER TWENTY-FOUR

1: C*nts are always the victim.

2: C*nts bring trouble upon other c*nts.

3: A lot of c*nts enjoy the harvest and know nothing about tilling and sowing.

4: C*nts use false weights and measures.

5: A c*nt believes justice is the exclusive province of the c*nt.

6: Obligation for you; irresponsibility for the c*nt.

7: Give a c*nt a child until the child is six and you will have two c*nts.

8: Unable to restrain their own c*ntishness; the c*nt is master of the world.

9: All rights and no responsibilities? C*nt.

10: What sort of a c*nt makes a c*nt out of another c*nt?

A moment of reflection.

Is it possible that you have ever made a c*nt out of someone else?

NOTES

CHAPTER TWENTY-FIVE

1: A lot of c*nts die young.

2: If you want honey don't make a c*nt of yourself by kicking over the beehive.

3: C*nty tradesman take deposits and never return.

4: When a c*nt dies some other c*nt is always eager to tell the world, what a c*nt the dead c*nt was.

5: Accepting the advice of a c*nt? Drink from the fountain of death.

6: A c*nt has winged ankles when c*ntishness is afoot.

7: Some rich c*nts believe money will keep them safe from the consequences of their c*ntishness.

8: Some c*nts would steal the air.

9: "I'll pay you back every penny" — lie of the c*nt.

10: Only silly c*nts believe the rich pay attention to the votes of the poor.

CHAPTER TWENTY-SIX

1: What is the c*nts is the c*nts. What is yours is the c*nts.

2: A c*nt is always scheming c*ntish things.

3: C*nts only express regret when faced with consequences.

4: "My c*ntish kids have special needs and must be supported by other c*nts. Other c*ntish kids are the monstrous progeny of c*ntish parents and are a waste of time and money!" Thinks the c*nt.

5: C*nts mourning a dead c*nt? Quickly over.

6: A c*nt will borrow money for diversion and entertainment.

7: Some rich c*nts believe money will keep them safe from the consequences of their c*ntishness. In a world of c*nts, the rich c*nt is probably right.

8: A crooked c*nt who makes a fortune is likely to be cheated out of it by another crooked c*nt. Unless they are c*nt enough to get away with it. Usually with the help of another bunch of crooked c*nt accomplices.

9: No matter what has been done for a c*nt in the past. If called upon for help the c*nt will not answer.

10: If you are a c*nt is that because you were trained to be a c*nt?

CHAPTER TWENTY-SEVEN

1: C*nts may be lamented but are never missed.

2: A c*nt is deaf to the cry of the oppressed.

3: A lot of c*nts live long lives of c*ntishness.

4: All that may be learned from a c*nt is c*ntishness.

5: C*ntish kids make c*nts of their parents.

6: If a c*nt is making a c*nt of themself — don't be afraid to give the c*nt a slap. You may save the c*nts life!

7: With disorder at home the c*nt seeks to set the world to rights.

8: C*nts love only themselves.

9: C*ntish lawyers have no interest in justice.

10: What sort of c*nt believes he can solve the problems of the developing world after watching Slumdog Millionaire?

CHAPTER TWENTY-EIGHT

1: For how long does a bunch of mourning c*nts actually mourn the dead c*nt — if at all?

2: Any good a c*nt does is a doorway to c*ntishness.

3: C*nts are generous with ridicule.

4: A greedy c*nt is a greedy c*nt is a greedy c*nt.

5: The love of money without wanting to work for it is c*ntish.

6: Jewellery on a c*nt is like putting a gold ring through a pig's snout.

7: C*nty kids cannot share the felt tips.

8: Never stand surety for a c*nt. You will lose what you have!

9: A crooked c*nt who makes a fortune is likely to be cheated out of it by another crooked c*nt. Unless they are c*nt enough to get away with it.

10: Everyone expects bullshit. Only c*nts accept it.

CHAPTER TWENTY-NINE

1: A c*nt in the classroom can learn nothing.

2: C*nts rejoice in their own c*ntishness.

3: When a c*nt dies a lot of other c*nts breathe a sigh of relief.

4: C*nts are always eager to act the c*nt.

5: Some c*nts use other c*nt's children as tools for intimidation.

6: C*nts never praise.

7: Stupid c*nts shout out their ignorance.

8: Even when thoroughly disliked; some c*nts believe themselves loved.

9: C*nts have shed so many tears for themselves they have none left for others.

10: C*nts wage war but dodge the draft.

CHAPTER THIRTY

1: C*nts are like diamonds. Many faced.

2: A c*nt shits in the river. A real c*nt goes upstream first.

3: A c*nt with knowledge will keep it to themselves.

4: A c*nt loves the smell of burning c*nt.

5: If you need to save a c*nts life with a slap; try not to be a c*nt about it.

6: The gratitude of a c*nt is a prelude to more favours being requested.

7: C*nts never weather a storm. They always blow away.

8: A c*nt is happy to "swear on the Bible".

9: Be careful what sort of c*nt you share good news with.

10: For how long does a c*nt have to act the c*nt before he becomes an actual c*nt?

A moment of reflection.
Who was the biggest c*nt of a teacher that you had at school?
NOTES

CHAPTER THIRTY – ONE

1: When a c*nt is unlucky it is the deliberate fault of other c*nts.

2: 100% of fuck all is still fuck all. Stupid c*nt!

3: True love is rare. The love of a c*nt? Non-existent.

4: C*nts lurk on the streets. They are at every corner.

5: The c*nt judges merit by immediate utility.

6: Be careful what sort of c*nt you share bad news with.

7: A c*nt can always see the beam in the other c*nts eye.

8: A c*nt will "swear on a stack of Bibles".

9: C*nts trick? Robbing the passer-by.

10: How does a c*nt learn their c*ntishness?

CHAPTER THIRTY – TWO

1: Keep wise company and you will become wise. Keep c*ntish company and you will be made a c*nt of.

2: A lucky c*nt takes credit for foresight and planning.

3: C*nts use learning to upgrade their c*ntishness.

4: A c*nt is like acid on an open wound.

5: The devious and treacherous nature of the c*nt will cause them to try to ruin you.

6: A c*nt that knows it is impossible to walk barefoot over broken glass will try to talk another c*nt into it.
7: C*nts prefer to display what they know: rather than learn what they do not.
8: C*nts run when found out.
9: C*nt's charity? Tax break.
10: The amorous embrace of a c*nt is the death grip of the constrictor.

CHAPTER THIRTY – THREE

1: A c*nt will offer to swear on their "mother's graves".

2: A married c*nt that's out to bed another c*nt is up to c*ntish tricks.

3: Peace treaties between two sets of c*nts spells trouble for a third set

4: C*nts trick? Child abuse.

5: See a sneer? Looking at a c*nt.

6: A c*nt preoccupied with their own merits sneers at the possibility of there being any merit in others.

7: A c*nt will say that you are their best friend ever – just before they make a c*nt of you.

8: C*nts do not feel shame

9: How can a c*nt have a friend in a world of c*nts?

10 Why do so many misguided c*nts have access to guided missiles?

CHAPTER THIRTY – FOUR

1: Ask a c*nt to reciprocate on an earlier favour. See what happens – bring an extra hankie.

2: Father of a c*nt: son of a c*nt?

3: When you get a c*nt out of your life beware lest they sniff their way back in.

4: Some c*nts like to make themselves seem tall by beheading other c*nts.

5: Children that act the c*nt make c*nts of their parents.

6: Whenever it suits a c*nt's c*ntish schemes they will abandon their companion without hesitation. In spite of all the avowals of perpetual fidelity.

7: C*nts always want to cast the first stone.

8: C*nts prefer filling their pockets over filling their heads.

9: Some c*nts are constantly seeking a handout.

10: C*nts cause famine; not climate.

CHAPTER THIRTY – FIVE

1: A c*nt will offer to swear on their "kid's lives".

2: A c*nt can never be a friend.

3: When a c*nt tells you they are your friend. Run for the hills.

4: Never lend your keys to a c*nt.

5: On divorce some c*nt will use the kids to make a c*nt of the other c*nt.

6: C*nts see deceit in honesty.

7: The c*nt expects other c*nts to forgive and forget.

8: Son of a c*nt: father of a c*nt?

9: What sort of a c*nt lets another c*nt talk them into walking barefoot over broken glass?

10: C*nts are often troubled by the terrors of the night.

CHAPTER THIRTY – SIX

1: A lot of c*nts would rather die than think.

2: Some c*nts can only see the finger; not the stars it points to.

3: A lot of c*nts give up their individuality because they don't believe they have any.

4: A c*ntish society often sends petty thieves to prison and promotes great thieves to high office.

5: There are a lot of c*nts out there that are sincerely ignorant and conscientiously stupid.

6: Some stupid c*nts will fall for anything and stand for nothing.

7: It is the c*nts with the most guns that call for gun control.

8: C*nts choose tyranny over conversation.

9: Lemming-like c*nts call the one walking away from the cliff's edge "C*nt!"

10: C*nts make decisions based on personal gain rather than universal values.

CHAPTER THIRTY – SEVEN

1: C*nts want the reward but not the labour.
2: It is a c*nts trick to raise prices when there are shortages.
3: A c*nt believes their achievements are the consequence of talent and hard work. The success of other c*nts is due to "connections".
4: A c*nt hates favourites but loves favour.
5: Weak c*nts are drawn to the c*ntishness of the powerful.
6: C*nts take the penny.
7: C*nts cheat the taxman: but greedily use the benefits.

8: C*nts choose war over peace.
9: Some c*nts believe big-pharma is more interested in cures than profits.
10: "Just following orders" excuse of the kapo-c*nt.

CHAPTER THIRTY – EIGHT

1: C*nts love things and use people.

2: A lot of c*nts waste their todays in the hope of buying a better tomorrow.

3: In the age of information, a lot of c*nts choose ignorance.

4: Some people believe they are depressed when really, they are just surrounded by c*nts.

5: Realize that if someone treats you like shit; they, not you, are the c*nt.

6: Some c*nts are more offended by "bad language" than evil deeds.

7: Big media events are there to distract c*nts from the big story.

8: Some c*nts prefer to fight over who created the world than oppose those that are destroying it.

9: C*nts end up with what they put up with.

10: If every c*nt is taught the same thing; how can any c*nt be expected to think differently?

CHAPTER THIRTY – NINE

1: C*nts prefer to be part of the problem than part of the solution.

2: C*nts always have a "get rich quick scheme".

3: C*nts leave those responsible for creating the problem in charge of finding the solution.

4: Some c*nts measure civilisation by how high it can build concrete.

5: Some c*nts are happiest when they are deceiving themselves.

6: C*nts with big armies often call c*nts with small armies "terrorists".

7: A c*nt that chooses "neutrality" is often siding with the oppressor.

8: C*nts that live a lie hate those that speak truth.

9: If you cannot control your own mind be sure that some other c*nt will.

10: Some c*nts would rather bomb the world than feed it.

CHAPTER FORTY

1: Small minded c*nts use words like "impossible".

2: Some c*nts believe they are free because they can't see the fences.

3: Some c*nts have a lot of education and little common sense.

4: Most political c*nts are bought and paid for.

5: A lot of c*nts are so busy trying to be normal they never get to be amazing.

6: If you are a c*nt is that because you were brought up by a c*nt?

7: A c*nt accepts the world they are given; rather than try to improve it.

8: Consider how c*ntish the average c*nt is. Then realize that half the c*nts in the world are even more c*ntish.

9: A lot of c*nts know how to make a living; but not a life.

10: C*ntishness is like booze. The more you have the less you see its effects.

CHAPTER FORTY – ONE

1: Crooked c*nts often act c*ntishly when dividing the proceeds.

2: C*nts like to inflict their pain on everyone else.

3: C*ntishness often hides behind counterfeit humility.

4: "Everyone is a c*nt but I am wise" thinks the c*nt.

5: C*nts favour short term gain over long term consequences.

6: A lot of c*nts are disabled by welfare.

7: It is easier to fool a c*nt than to convince a c*nt that they are being fooled.

8: What sort of a celebrity c*nt preaches about the environment from their private jet?

9: C*nts are happy to bury the hatchet — as long as it is in some other c*nt's back.

10: Some c*nts just enjoy watching the world burn.

HUNT THE C*NT

C	*	N	T	*	T	N	*	C	C
*	C	*	N	T	N	*	C	*	*
N	T	C	*	N	T	C	N	N	N
T	N	*	C	T	C	T	C	T	T
C	*	N	T	N	*	C	*	N	T
T	C	T	C	*	N	T	T	N	T
N	T	N	*	C	T	N	*	C	N
*	N	C	N	*	*	C	*	*	*
C	*	N	T	N	C	N	T	N	C
*	C	*	N	T	*	T	T	T	T

And another baby dies and another angel cries.

Bunch of C*nts!!!

FOR MORE FROM

THE LITTLE BOOK OF C*NTS

FIND AND FOLLOW US ON FACEBOOK

and

littlebookofc.nts@gmail.com

COMING SOON

THE LITTLE BOOK OF
C*NTS GOES TO THE
MOVIES !!!!

www.ingramcontent.com/pod-product-compliance
Lightning Source LLC
LaVergne TN
LVHW051704080426
835511LV00017B/2723